FIRST
NATURE
Activ
BOOK

Angela Wilkes

LONDON, NEW YORK, MELBOURNE, MUNICH, and DELHI

Art editor Chris Scollen
Photography Dave King
Senior designer Neville Graham
Senior editors Marie Greenwood,
Sue Nicholson
Production Amy Bennett

DK Delhi
Senior Editor Glenda Fernandes
Senior Designer Shefali Upadhyay
Designer Mini Dhawan
DTP Designer Harish Aggarwal

First published in Great Britain as
My First Nature Book in 1990
This revised edition published in 2007
by Dorling Kindersley Limited,
80 Strand, London WC2R 0RL

2 4 6 8 10 9 7 5 3 1
MD371 - 10/06

A CIP catalogue record for this book is available from
the British Library.

ISBN 978-1-40531-957-7

Reproduced by Media Development
and Printing Ltd, UK
Printed and bound by Leo Paper Products Ltd, China

**Discover more at
www.dk.com**

CONTENTS

NATURE IN PICTURES

My First Nature Book is full of interesting things to do that will help you to find out more about nature. Simple step-by-step instructions show you what to do and there are photographs of everything you need to collect and of the finished projects. At the back of the book you can find tear-out sheets of blotting paper. Use them to sprout seeds (see page 14) or press flowers (see page 36).

How to use this book

Equipment
These illustrated checklists show you which pieces of equipment to have ready before you start a project.

The things you need
The things to collect for each project are shown clearly, to help you check you have everything you need.

Step-by-step
Step-by-step photographs and clear instructions show you exactly what to do at every stage of the project.

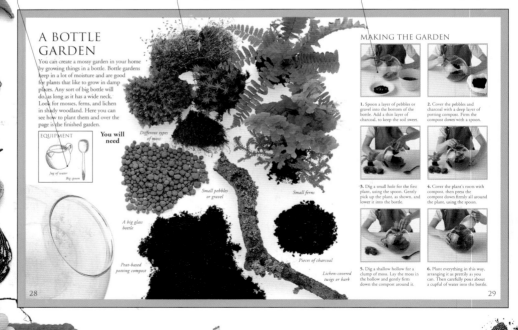

A BOTTLE GARDEN
You can create a mossy garden in your home by growing things in a bottle. Bottle gardens keep in a lot of moisture and are good for plants that like to grow in damp places. Any sort of big bottle will do, as long as it has a wide neck. Look for mosses, ferns, and lichen in shady woodland. Here you can see how to plant them and over the page is the finished garden.

EQUIPMENT
Jug of water
Big spoon

You will need

Different types of moss

Small pebbles or gravel

Small ferns

A big glass bottle

Peat-based potting compost

Pieces of charcoal

Lichen-covered twigs or bark

MAKING THE GARDEN

1. Spoon a layer of pebbles or gravel into the bottom of the bottle. Add a thin layer of charcoal, to keep the soil sweet.

2. Cover the pebbles and charcoal with a deep layer of potting compost. Firm the compost down with a spoon.

3. Dig a small hole for the first plant, using the spoon. Gently pick up the plant, as shown, and lower it into the bottle.

4. Cover the plant's roots with compost, then press the compost down firmly all around the plant, using the spoon.

5. Dig a shallow hollow for a clump of moss. Lay the moss in the hollow and gently firm down the compost around it.

6. Plant everything in this way, arranging it as prettily as you can. Then carefully pour about a cupful of water into the bottle.

28

29

Things to remember

- Read the instructions before you begin. Some projects need to be done outdoors and some indoors.
- Put on an apron or old shirt, and roll up your sleeves.
- Cover your work table with paper before you start a project.
- Gather together everything you need before you start.
- Follow the Country Code on page 48.
- Don't forget to water your plants and take good care of your animals.
- When you have finished a project, put everything away.

Collecting outdoors
The pictures of things to collect are only a guideline. The things you find may not look exactly the same.

The final results
Large pictures show you what finished projects look like, making it easy for you to copy them.

Aftercare
Many of the projects have step-by-step instructions showing you how to care for your plants or creatures.

WORLD IN A BOTTLE

Mosses and ferns are happiest in damp, shady places, so put the bottle garden in a cool place where the light is good, but not bright. It is best to avoid direct sunlight. Once you have made the garden, it should need very little looking after. You can see what to do on the opposite page.

Watch the mosses and ferns to see how they grow or change. In spring, the mosses may grow tiny grass-like stems with capsules on them. These capsules contain the mosses' spores, which are like seeds. You can see three different types of moss with spore capsules at the bottom of the bottle garden here. Ferns also produce spore capsules. They are usually on the undersides of the leaves.

Small fern

Twig covered with lichen. Although moss and lichen look alike, they are not related. Lichen is a special type of fungus.

EQUIPMENT

Scissors

Water spray

Moss with spore capsules

30

Maidenhair fern

Potting compost

Moss with spore capsules

Moss

Watering the garden

Your bottle garden will need very little watering. Just spray it with water occasionally, to keep the compost moist.

Pruning

Keep an eye on the condition of your plants. Snip any dead leaves or pieces of fern with a small pair of scissors.

Open or closed?

Leave the bottle open until there are no drops of water left on the inside of the glass. Then you can put the lid on.

31

NATURE SPOTTER'S KIT

Finding out about nature is all about using your eyes. The more carefully you look at things, the more you will find out. It helps to make notes of everything you see. You will also need to collect things, so that you can compare them. Here are the basic things you will need for your nature expeditions.

Small envelopes, for collecting seeds

Plastic bags and ties, for plant specimens

Elastic bands

Sticky labels, for labelling your finds

Small magnifying glass

Containers with holes in their lids or with muslin covers, for collecting insects

Tweezers, for picking up delicate objects

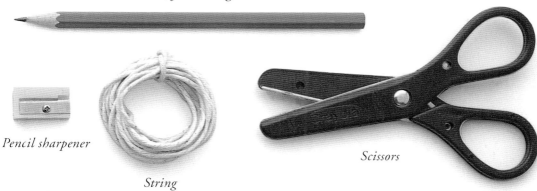

Pencil, for making notes

Pencil sharpener

String

Scissors

Paintbrush, for picking up caterpillars

Coloured pencils

Nature diary (see page 46)

7

A NATURE MUSEUM

Your nature collections will look impressive if displayed well so why not make your own nature showcases to show off the interesting things you find? Here you can find out how to make a simple showcase, and on the next page, how to display a collection in the finished showcase.

Cotton wool

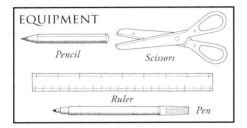

EQUIPMENT

Pencil

Scissors

Ruler

Pen

You will need

Glue stick

Clean sand

MAKING THE SHOWCASE

Glue three of the matchboxes together, side by side, in a row. Glue the other three matchboxes together in the same way.

Glue the two rows of three matchboxes together. As each matchbox has a partition, you will now have 12 compartments.

If you want to make a bigger compartment, glue down the partition in the middle of one of the matchboxes.

*Thin card,
for labels*

*Thick,
coloured
card*

Six empty household size boxes of matches

Cut out a piece of thick card about 3 cm wider and 3 cm longer than the showcase *. Glue the showcase in the centre of it.

Put a thin layer of cotton wool into each compartment in the showcase. You could use sand for a showcase of a seaside collection.

For labels, cut out rectangles of thin card. Fold them in half and glue them to the partitions between the matchboxes.

* Ask an adult to help you.

9

NATURE SHOWCASES

Use your nature showcases to show off your most treasured finds. You may have a special collection of feathers, stones, or leaves. Or you may have a seaside or woodland collection. Arrange your exhibits so that similar things are grouped together, and label them, if you can.

Rock collection
Look for rocks and pebbles on a beach or riverbank, or on a mountain. You can find them in all colours and with all sorts of patterns. Look them up in a book to find out what they are called.

Beachcomber's showcase

Beachcombing can reward you with all kinds of treasures for a showcase. The best place to look is along the high tide mark, especially after a storm. You can find shells in all shapes and sizes, seaweeds, and strange pieces of driftwood.

When you get home, clean your finds under a running water tap with an old toothbrush. Let them dry thoroughly before putting them in your showcase. Carry on the seaside theme by lining the showcase with sand, rather than with cotton wool.

COLLECTING SEEDS

Seeds come in all shapes and sizes. Some are as fine as dust and others look like stones. Some are encased in a juicy fruit; others have their own parachutes. Many flowers, trees, vegetables, fruits, and grasses grow from seeds. See how many different kinds of seeds you can collect. Below are some to look for.

Seeds to collect

Acorns (from oak trees)

Tree seeds
The best time to collect tree seeds is early autumn, when they have just fallen from the trees. If you leave it too late, many seeds will have been eaten by birds and animals.

EQUIPMENT

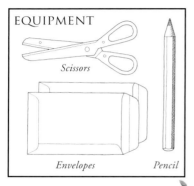

Scissors

Envelopes   *Pencil*

Maple seeds

Horse chestnuts

Seeds in pine cones

Grass seed and grains
Collect different types of seeds from wild grasses or from grains like wheat.

Flower seeds
Look for flower seeds once the petals have died and a seed head has formed.

Thistledown

Wheat

Wild grasses

Poppy seeds

Vegetable seeds

All the different kinds of dried beans and peas are seeds.
Soak them for 24 hours before planting them.

Runner beans

Black-eyed beans

Aduki beans

Flageolet beans

Fruit seeds

Cut fruit in half to find the seeds*. Some
types of fruit have pips and others stones.

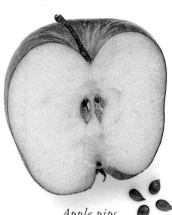

Lemon pips

Avocado stone

Apple pips

Grape pips

HARVESTING FLOWER SEEDS

Cut a flower when the petals have died. Hold the flower upside down and shake the seeds on to a piece of paper.

Fold the piece of paper as shown and pour the flower seeds into a small envelope. Use one envelope for each type of seed.

Seal the envelope and label it clearly. Keep it in a dark, dry drawer if you are keeping the seeds to plant in spring.

*Be careful with sharp knives. Ask an adult to help you.

SPROUTING SEEDS

Plant some of the seeds you have collected and watch how they grow. Most seeds will sprout if they have enough light, air, and water. On the right you can find out how to plant pips and seeds. Turn the page to see how they grow.

You will need

For growing beans

Large dried beans*

For cress heads

Blotting paper – use the sheets at the back of the book.

Cress seeds

For planting seeds

Egg shells

Large plastic bags and ties

Pips or seeds

Plant labels

Cotton wool

Seed compost

EQUIPMENT

Bowl

Scissors

Pencil

Knife

Jam jar   Flower pots   Paint box

Trowel   Jug of water

* You can use any kind of dried bean.

CRESS HEADS

Draw or paint a simple face on each of the broken egg shells. Stand the egg shell faces in an egg carton, to keep them steady.

Dip balls of cotton wool in a bowl of water so that they are completely soaked. Fill the egg shells with wet cotton wool.

Sprinkle cress seed over the cotton wool. Put the eggs on a window sill and wait for a few days. Keep the cotton wool moist.

SHOOTING BEANS

Cut out a piece of blotting paper tall enough to fill your jam jar from top to bottom, and long enough to go right round it.

Roll the blotting paper into a narrow tube and slide it into the jam jar. The blotting paper will open out to fill the jar.

Push a few beans down between the paper and the jar. Pour a little water into the jar, then put it on a window sill.

PLANTING PIPS AND SEEDS

Put some seed compost in a bowl and water it, to make it moist. Stir well with a trowel. Fill some small pots with the compost.

Plant different pips or seeds in each pot. Push them about 1 cm down into the compost. Label each pot, to say what is in it.

Put each flower pot inside a polythene bag and tie the top*. Put the pots in a warm place and wait to see which seeds sprout.

*The polythene bags act like mini-greenhouses or incubators.

WATCH SEEDS GROW

Look at your pips, seeds, and beans every day and you will be able to watch each stage of their growth at close hand. You will find that some things grow very quickly, but others take longer. Remember to water your seeds and seedlings if they look dry. It is also a good idea to turn them regularly, to help them grow straight. All plants are delicate, so treat them with care and they will grow healthy and strong.

Baby tree

PIPS AND SEEDS

Here you can see some tree seeds and marrow pips growing. The tree seeds were planted in autumn and kept in a cool place all winter. The marrow pips were planted 10 days before the picture was taken.

Baby tree

CRESS HEADS

Watch how the little faces grow green hair! Keep the cotton wool moist and the cress will take about 10 days to grow. Then you can cut it and add it to salads or egg sandwiches.

Marrow seedlings

SHOOTING BEANS

Here you can see how a bean grows. First, the bean swells and the hard outer skin splits (1). Next, a tiny root appears (2).

The root grows downwards and a shoot starts to emerge (3). The shoot then grows upwards. Rootlets begin to grow out from the root and the plant produces leaves (4).

From now on, the bean plant grows fast (5). When it is too big for the jar, plant it in a pot or in the garden, with a stick to support it.

1.

2.

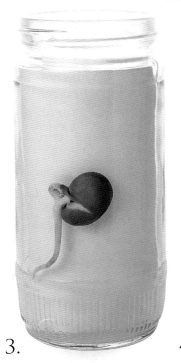

3.

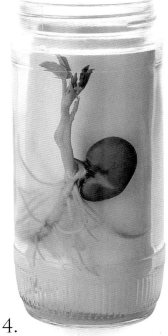

4.

5.

FEEDING THE BIRDS

Feeding the birds in winter helps them to survive when food is scarce and gives you a chance to watch them. Here you can find out how to make a filling bird pudding and peanut kebabs. The quantities given for the pudding will fill a small yogurt pot. Turn the page to see other tasty ideas for your birds' menu.

125 g of any of these kitchen scraps:

Porridge oats

Leftover cooked vegetables

You will need

60 g cooking fat

Birdseed

Cooked rice

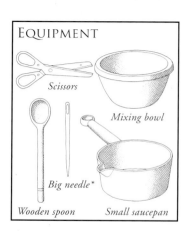
Mixed nuts

Brown breadcrumbs

Small twig

Grated cheese

EQUIPMENT

Scissors

Mixing bowl

Big needle*

Wooden spoon   *Small saucepan*

Yogurt pot

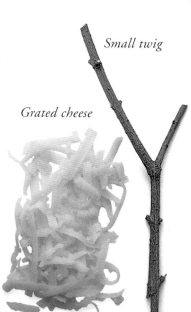

* Use a blunt-tipped darning needle

Big fir cone

For peanut kebabs

String   *Peanuts in their shells and any other nuts*

MAKING THE PUDDING

1. Mix the scraps together in the bowl. Leave aside some birdseed. Ask an adult to melt the lard in a saucepan over a low heat.

2. Pour the melted fat over the mixture of scraps in the bowl and stir everything together well with a wooden spoon.

3. Spoon the pudding mixture into the yogurt pot. Push a twig into the pudding, then leave the pudding to set hard.

4. When the pudding has set, pull it out of the yogurt pot by the twig and roll it in birdseed. Tie a piece of string to the twig.

Pine cone feeder

Push bird pudding into the cracks between the open scales of a big fir cone, then hang the cone from a piece of string.

Peanut kebab

Make holes in peanut shells and other nuts with a big needle*. Knot one end of a piece of string, then thread the nuts on to it.

* Be careful with the needle.   **19**

BIRDS' MENU

Here are some ideas for simple bird feeders and titbits. Hang the feeders where you can watch them easily, and make sure they are out of reach of cats. Keep a record in your nature diary (see page 46) of all the birds that use the feeders. Do the same birds keep coming back, and do they have regular feeding times?

SCRAP BAG

You can make a very simple feeder for the birds from a fine mesh fruit bag*. Fill it with nuts or bird pudding, then tie the top with a piece of string and hang it up.

COCONUT BELL

Hang half a coconut upside down from a piece of string and agile birds will peck out all the coconut. When the shell is empty, fill it with bird pudding.

TIT BELL

This is the finished bird pudding you saw how to make on the last two pages.

*Usually available at supermarkets.

PEANUT KEBAB
String up your peanut kebab (see page 19) and watch the tits and finches break open the nuts.

FIR CONE FEEDER
This is the feeder you saw how to make on page 19. Watch the birds sway from it as they feed.

FEEDING LOG
You will need an adult to help you make this. Ask him or her to drill holes in the log and to screw a hook in the top. Fill the holes with bird pudding and hang up the log. Woodpeckers may come to peck out the pudding.

TREEPRINTS

A tree's bark is its skin and, like human fingerprints, no two trees have identical bark. Different types of tree also have different bark, and bark also changes as a tree grows older. You can keep a record of what sort of bark a tree has by taking a rubbing of it. This way you can build up a file of "treeprints". Here you can see what to do.

Drawing pins

You will need

Fat wax crayons

Masking tape

Pieces of thin, strong paper, about 30 cm by 30 cm

WHAT TO DO

Choose a tree with fairly smooth bark, with no moss or lichen growing on it. Tape or pin a piece of paper firmly on to the tree.

Using the flat side of a wax crayon, rub firmly up and down the paper. Keep doing this until the paper is covered.

Untape the paper from the tree. Write the name of the tree on the back of the paper, if you know what it is called.

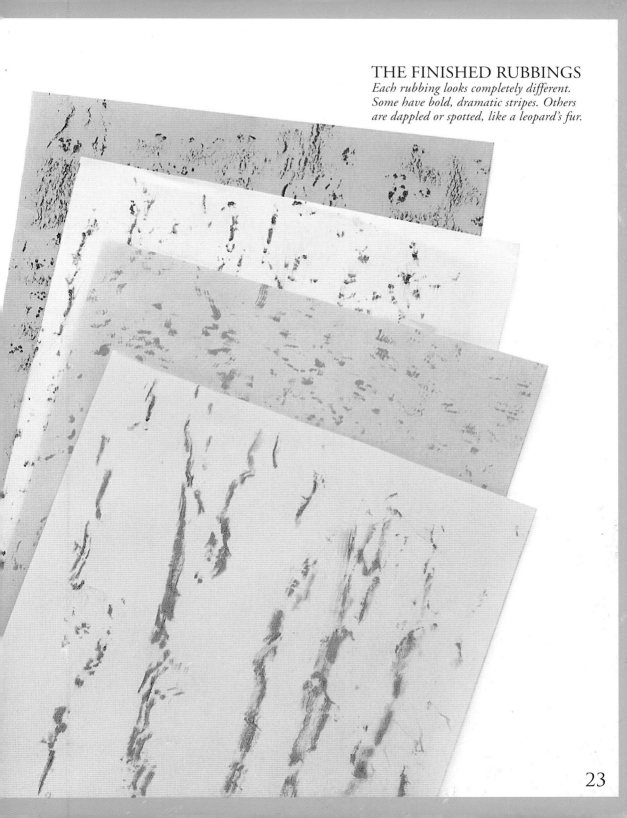

THE FINISHED RUBBINGS
*Each rubbing looks completely different.
Some have bold, dramatic stripes. Others
are dappled or spotted, like a leopard's fur.*

23

FROM BUD TO LEAF

Most broadleaved trees have no leaves in winter and look lifeless. But look closely at some twigs and you will see that each one is already covered in tiny buds. These buds contain the beginnings of next year's shoots, leaves, and flowers. You can make buds open early by cutting some twigs and bringing them indoors. Put them in a jar of water and you can watch how they burst into life. The best twigs to try are horse chestnut, forsythia, and magnolia. Here you can see how horse chestnut buds open.

OPENING BUDS

Side twig

Each fat bud is covered with sticky scales that protect it. Inside the scales are tightly packed new stems and leaves.

This is a girdle scar. You can tell how old the twig is by counting the girdle scars.

Leaf scar from last year.

The buds swell and begin to burst out of the scales.

The new leaves inside the buds begin to unfurl. They are covered in protective fluffy down.

Tiny flower covered in down.

The stems start to grow and the leaves open out to the light.

Flower

Flower

New shoot

The bud scales curl back. In a few weeks they will drop off, leaving a girdle scar.

CREEPY CRAWLY PIT TRAPS

You do not have to go far to find animals to watch. There are tiny creatures all around you in your garden or park. To find out what they are, set up simple pit traps. Check the traps often and write down what you find, to keep a record of local wildlife.

You will need (for each trap)

A piece of wood or a tile

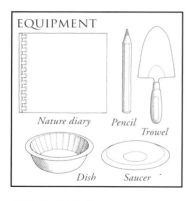

EQUIPMENT

Nature diary *Pencil* *Trowel* *Dish* *Saucer*

Four stones

A yogurt pot or jam jar

Food for bait

A cube of cheese   *Biscuit crumbs*   *A piece of apple*   *A piece of meat*

SETTING UP A PIT TRAP

Dig a hole in the garden. Sink the yogurt pot into it, so that its rim is level with the soil. Fill in soil around the edges of the pot.

Drop a small piece of cheese or other bait into the yogurt pot trap. The smell of the bait will attract small creatures to the trap.

Put the four stones around the top of the yogurt pot. Lay the piece of wood across them to make a protective cover for the trap.

INSECT PATROL

Empty the creatures in the trap into a dish. Write down what you have caught in your nature diary, then set the creatures free.

Try setting several traps, using different baits, such as meat, fish, or fruit. Do different types of bait attract different creatures?

To see which creatures live where, sink traps in different places: in a flowerbed or vegetable plot, for example.

The pit trap

Here you can see right into a pit trap. Small creatures have fallen into it and cannot climb out up the slippery sides. Check your traps every few hours, to see whether any creatures have fallen into them.

The cover of the pit trap protects the insects inside it from bright sun, the rain, or any hungry animals on the prowl.

Ground level

Stone

Bait

Yogurt pot

Creatures caught in the trap

A BOTTLE GARDEN

You can create a mossy garden in your home by growing things in a bottle. Bottle gardens keep in a lot of moisture and are good for plants that like to grow in damp places. Any sort of big bottle will do, as long as it has a wide neck. Look for mosses, ferns, and lichen in shady woodland. Here you can see how to plant them and over the page is the finished garden.

EQUIPMENT

Jug of water

Big spoon

You will need

Different types of moss

Small pebbles or gravel

A big glass bottle

Peat-based potting compost

MAKING THE GARDEN

1. Spoon a layer of pebbles or gravel into the bottom of the bottle. Add a thin layer of charcoal to keep the soil sweet.

2. Cover the pebbles and charcoal with a deep layer of potting compost. Firm the compost down with a spoon.

3. Dig a small hole for the first plant, using the spoon. Gently pick up the plant, as shown, and lower it into the bottle.

4. Cover the plant's roots with compost, then press the compost down firmly all around the plant, using the spoon.

5. Dig a shallow hollow for a clump of moss. Lay the moss in the hollow and gently firm down the compost around it.

6. Plant everything in this way, arranging it as prettily as you can. Then carefully pour about a cupful of water into the bottle.

Small ferns

Pieces of charcoal

Lichen-covered twigs or bark

29

WORLD IN A BOTTLE

Mosses and ferns are happiest in damp, shady places, so put the bottle garden in a cool place where the light is good, but not bright. It is best to avoid direct sunlight.

Once you have made the garden, it should need very little looking after. You can see what to do on the opposite page.

Watch the mosses and ferns to see how they grow or change. In spring, the mosses may grow tiny grass-like stems with capsules on them. These capsules contain the mosses' spores, which are like seeds. You can see three different types of moss with spore capsules at the bottom of the bottle garden here. Ferns also produce spore capsules. They are usually on the undersides of the leaves.

Small fern

Twig covered with lichen. Although moss and lichen look alike, they are not related. Lichen is a special type of fungus.

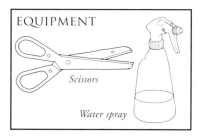

EQUIPMENT

Scissors

Water spray

Moss with spore capsules

30

Maidenhair fern

Potting compost

Moss with spore capsules

Moss

Watering the garden

Your bottle garden will need very little watering. Just spray it with water occasionally, to keep the compost moist.

Pruning

Keep an eye on the condition of your plants. Snip off any dead leaves or pieces of fern with a small pair of scissors.

Open or closed?

Leave the bottle open until there are no drops of water left on the inside of the glass. Then you can put the lid on.

31

CATERPILLAR HOUSE

Keep some caterpillars and you
may be lucky enough to see how
they change into butterflies.
Look for caterpillars on the
leaves of plants and bushes
in spring and summer. The
plant they are on is probably
their food plant, so pick plenty
of leaves for them to eat. Here
and on pages 34 and 35 you
can find out how to make a
home for your wriggly pets.

You will need

Caterpillars

EQUIPMENT

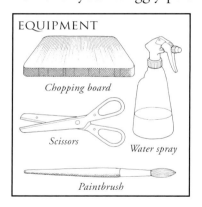

Chopping board

Scissors

Water spray

Paintbrush

MAKING THE CATERPILLAR HOUSE

Ask an adult to cut a big hole
out of the lid of the plastic
container, leaving just a bit of
the lid inside the rim.

Cut out a piece of muslin that is
big enough to cover the top of
the container and overlap the
edges all the way round.

Line the container with over-
lapping pieces of kitchen paper
or tissues. Spray them lightly
with water, to dampen them.

A large plastic container

Kitchen paper or tissues

A big piece of muslin

Small twigs

The leaves your caterpillars eat

Lay the food leaves (leaves from the plant on which you found the caterpillars) in the container. Lay the twigs on top.

One at a time, gently pick up the caterpillars on the paintbrush and put them carefully on the leaves in the container.

Lay the muslin over the top of the container. Then push the lid down over the muslin, to hold it firmly in place.

Turn the page to see what to do next. 33

FROM CATERPILLAR TO BUTTERFLY

Here is the caterpillar house without its lid, so that you can see inside. You will be able to watch your caterpillars change into chrysalises when they are fully grown, and later into butterflies. Keep the caterpillar house in a quiet place away from direct sunlight. Caterpillars eat a lot, so clean out the house and give them fresh leaves to eat every day. On the right you can find out what to do.

Kitchen paper

CATERPILLAR FOOD
The caterpillars shown here eat passionflower leaves and nothing else. Each type of caterpillar has its own food plant, so it is very important that you give them the right leaves to eat. These are usually the leaves on which you found them in the wild.

CATERPILLARS
Caterpillars are very delicate. Do not prod or disturb them, because you could easily harm them. As caterpillars grow bigger, they outgrow their skins and moult, so do not worry if you see a caterpillar wriggle out of its skin. Most caterpillars moult several times during their lives.

Plastic container

THE CHRYSALIS STAGE

This is a chrysalis (or pupa). A caterpillar changes into a chrysalis when it is fully grown. The chrysalis is its last skin change before it becomes a butterfly (or moth). The chrysalis may form on a twig or on the side of the container. Try not to disturb it. You may have to wait a long time before the butterfly emerges.

CLEANING OUT THE HOUSE

Take the lid off the caterpillar house and carefully lift out everything inside, including the kitchen paper.

Line the caterpillar house with clean kitchen paper or tissue and spray it with water to dampen it. Put in fresh food leaves.

Twig

Leaves

BUTTERFLIES

When a butterfly first emerges from a chrysalis, it will have folded-up wings and look rather strange. It will take several hours for its wings to dry and harden. A butterfly is very delicate, so leave it alone and set it free when it is sunny.

Pick up each caterpillar in turn on the paintbrush and put it back in the caterpillar house. Then put the lid back on.

35

PLANT PRESS

Pressing is a simple but magical way of preserving beautiful flowers and leaves so that they last forever. Flowers with flat faces, like pansies, primroses, and daisies are all easy to press. Pick dry, undamaged flowers and leaves and press them as quickly as you can, so that they keep their colour well *. Here you can find out how to make a simple plant press, and over the page you can see how to make pictures and cards.

You will need

Flowers and leaves to press

Forget-me-nots

Daisies

EQUIPMENT

Scissors

Heavy books

Never pick rare flowers. See page 48.

Violas

Primrose

Ivy leaves

Polyanthus

White blotting paper – use the tear-out sheets at the back of the book

Heavy books

WHAT TO DO

1. Open the book. Cut out a piece of blotting paper about the same size as the open book. Fold the paper in half, then open it out.

2. Lay the blotting paper across the book. Arrange the plants flat on the right half of the paper, leaving space between them.

3. Carefully fold the left side of the blotting paper over the plants. Then close the book over the blotting paper*.

4. Put some heavy books or magazines on top of the book, to weigh it down. Leave the plants to dry for at least four weeks.

* *To press more plants, do the same thing further on in the book.*

Turn the page to see what to do next. 37

EVERLASTING FLOWERS

After four weeks, your pressed plants should be dry and flat. You can glue them into your nature diary, to keep a record of what you have found, or make pictures with them. Start by making simple pictures with just one or two flowers, then experiment once you have had more practice. Here are some ideas for what you can make with your pressed flowers.

You will need

Thick paper or card

Cotton buds

Rubber-based glue

Pressed flowers and leaves

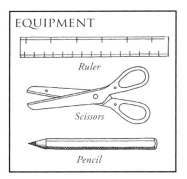

EQUIPMENT

Ruler

Scissors

Pencil

MAKING PICTURES

Measure and draw out the size you want your picture to be on the paper or card. Cut the paper out carefully.

Arrange where to put each flower and leaf. Pick up a flower and dab a tiny spot of glue on the back of it.

Gently position the flower where you want it. Do the same with the other flowers, then leave the glue to dry.

FLOWERY IDEAS

You can make your own unique cards, gift tags, or bookmarks using simple arrangements of pressed flowers and leaves.

Picture

Bookmark

Gift tags

A WORM FARM

Worms are busy creatures and play an important role in the garden, keeping the soil in good condition. You can watch what they do by making this simple worm farm. Keep it until you have seen what the worms do, then put them back where you found them.

You will need

*Earthworms**

A large glass jar

Dead leaves

Sand

EQUIPMENT

Trowel

Bowls

Water spray

Small bowl

Dark cloth

Sieved garden soil

The worms should be big mature ones with a "saddle" around the middle.

MAKING THE WORM FARM

Fill the jar with alternate layers of soil and sand. Make each layer about 2.5 cm deep and spray each one with water.

Gently put the worms into the jar, keeping them away from bright light. Five or six worms should be enough for a jar this size.

Cover the top layer of soil with dead leaves. Then cover the whole jar with a dark cloth or put in it a dark place*.

BURROWING WORMS

Leave the worm farm alone for a few days, then take a look at it. Here you can see how the worms have tunnelled through the soil and sand, so that the different layers have begun to mix together. They have also dragged the leaves down into the soil, to eat them.

Dead leaves

Soil

Layers of soil merging

USEFUL WORMS

Worms do not eat all the leaves and plant matter they pull down into the soil. Their leftovers help to enrich the soil and make better growing conditions for plants. The worm tunnels are also useful for plants, because they help to provide air for the plants' roots.

Leaves dragged down into soil

Sand

Worm tunnels

Worm

* The worms need to be in complete darkness so that they think they are underground.

41

PETWATCHING

You do not need to live on a farm or near a zoo to find out about animals and how they behave. You can learn all sorts of fascinating things by keeping a close watch on the pets you have at home. Your puppy will often behave in exactly the same way as a fox or wolf cub and your kitten will play like a lion cub.

Watch your pets carefully and write down the things you notice in your nature diary (see page 46). What does your pet do and where does it go? How can you tell what mood it is in? Keep your eyes open and you can learn a lot, not only about your pet, but about animals in general. Here are some things to look out for.

TAIL TALK
You can tell a lot about a cat's feelings by its tail. A happy cat walks with its tail held high. An angry cat may swish its tail from side to side. A frightened cat often cowers with its tail tucked between its legs.

EXPRESSIVE FACES
Watch your cat's face, to see what mood it is in. When curious, it will prick up its ears and open its eyes wide. It may also twitch its whiskers. When frightened or angry, it will lay its ears back flat.

PLAY-LEARNING
Playing is how your kitten learns skills that are important in the wild, such as hunting. Kittens love to chase and pounce on interesting new things. Watch how they use their paws to hook things towards them for a closer look.

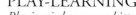

CAT STOPS
Watch where your cat goes every day. Most cats are creatures of habit and will have their own special look-out posts and places for resting, cleaning, or sunbathing. Your cat will also have its own prowling "territory" and will rarely venture outside it.

DOGGY MOODS

As with people, you can tell a lot about a dog's mood by the expression on its face. Dogs can look questioning or fierce and can even appear to smile. Learn which signs tell you when your dog is happy or sad, or when it wants to play.

NOSEY DOGS

A dog's sense of smell is more sensitive than ours and gives it all sorts of useful information. That is why dogs want to sniff everything wherever they go.

WOOFS AND WHIMPERS

Dogs make a whole range of sounds: whimpers, growls, snarls, and barks. Listen carefully to your dog and learn to recognize the different sounds and what they mean.

BODY LANGUAGE

A dog shows its feelings with its whole body, as well as its face. In particular, it has an expressive tail. Watch how your dog moves and what it does to show what it wants to do.

TRACKING YOUR PETS

An easy way to study animal tracks is to make plaster casts of them and the best places to look for tracks are in mud or wet sand. But before collecting different prints, why not practise by taking casts of your pet's paw prints? Here you can find out what to do.

You will need

Paper clips

Water

Plaster of Paris

EQUIPMENT

Old toothbrush

Old bowl

Old spoon

Trowel

Newspaper

Bottle (for carrying water)

Strips of thin card about 30 cm long and 5 cm wide

MAKING THE PLASTER CASTS

Find a print in wet mud. Clip a strip of card into a circle big enough to go round the print. Push it into the mud around the print.

Mix the plaster of Paris* in the bowl. Gently pour about 5 cm of plaster into the card ring. Leave it for 15 minutes, to set.

Dig up the plaster cast and the mud around it. Wrap the cast in newspaper and take it home. Leave it for a day, to set**.

Ask an adult to help you, following the instructions on the packet.
** Wash the bowl and spoon with warm water as soon as you get home.

PRINTS IN PLASTER
When the plaster is hard, unclip the card and scrub the cast clean under running water, using an old toothbrush. The finished cast will be a raised copy of your pet's pawprint. Here you can see plaster casts of dog and cat paw prints and of a guinea pig's tracks.

GUINEA PIG PRINT

CAT PAW PRINT

DOG PAW PRINT

YOUR NATURE DIARY

Keep a nature diary and it will become your own personal record of all the interesting things you see and find. You can use any notebook for your diary, but it is best if it has a hard cover and a ring binding, so that you can open it out flat when you are drawing.

Make notes in your nature diary of everything you see, and draw things as often as you can. You can keep records of how your seeds are growing and of what your pets are doing. If you can, label each find in your diary, and write down where you found everything.

FACTS FIRST
Start each entry in your diary with the date. Then you could say what the weather has been like and where you have been.

LEAVES AND FLOWERS
Your diary is a good place to keep leaves or flowers that you find. First you must press them (see pages 36 and 37). When they are flat and dry, glue them into the diary.

GROWING THINGS
Keep notes of how your seeds and plants are growing (see pages 14 to 17 for some ideas). Draw each new stage in your seedlings' growth and write down everything that you notice happening.

Sunday 9th April
Sunny day, some clouds. Went to the wood near Grandma's house.

Buddleia leaves

Horse chestnut leaf

My bean plant

The roots have tiny roots growing from them. The shoot has reached the top of the paper.

Polyanthus flower from garden.

FINDS

You can glue or tape interesting finds, like these feathers, in your diary. Write down when and where you found them and label them if you know what they are called.

QUICK SKETCHES

Try to draw new birds that you see. You do not have to be good at drawing. Draw two circles – one for the head and one for the body. Add the tail, beak and legs and a wing, then fill in the colours and details of special markings.

Pheasant feathers found in the wood.

Saturday 15th April
Seagull on playing field.

Black head

White flash on wing

Yellow beak

Pink belly

Grey and black tail

COUNTRY CODE

When collecting things, only take what you need
and make sure you leave plenty of specimens behind.

•

Leave things in the wild as you found them.

•

Do not drop litter anywhere.

•

Never disturb nesting birds or steal birds' eggs.

•

Be gentle with any creatures that you catch.
Set them free when you have finished a project.

•

Only pick wild flowers if there are plenty
growing, and just pick a few.
Never pick rare plants.